THE U.S. ECONOMY EXPOSED

DEBT CRISIS WHO DUNNIT?

THE U.S. ECONOMY EXPOSED

What Factors Caused the U. S. Debt Crisis

and

Who is at Fault?

A look back in the history of economic downturns and the Party in Control!

By
Keith Ouellette

TABLE OF CONTENTS

- Introduction - 1929 versus 2009

- Chapter 1 - A Fair Comparison?

- Chapter 2 - The New Deal

- Chapter 3 - A Closer Look!

- Chapter 4 - New Deal II?

- Chapter 5 - Private Investment

- The Final Chapter . . . *for now!*

Copyright Info

Copyright 2012 Kouell Publishing LLC All Rights Reserved. This book may not be reproduced or transmitted in any form without the express written permission of the Publisher. Every effort has been made to make the content of this book complete and accurate as possible. The opinions expressed by the Author are his own and we assume no responsibility or liability for errors, inaccuracies or omissions.

Macroeconomic theory is the practice of interpreting economic indicators and any combination thereof. Even highly-trained Economists express their own opinions, frequently misinterpret the data and err in their resulting forecasts. The Author is highly experienced in the financial services industry, but is not a subject matter expert (SME) specific to Macroeconomic Theory. The opinions expressed in this book are solely his own based on interpretation of the data obtained from U.S. Government Agencies and other sources identified in the Acknowledgments.

This book has been written to provide you with information to help you understand some of the factors that drive the U.S. economy. The purpose of this book is to educate. The author and publisher do not warrant that the information contained in this book is fully complete and shall not be responsible for any errors and omissions. The author and publisher shall have neither responsibility nor liability to any person or entity with respect to any loss or damage caused or alleged to be caused directly or indirectly by the contents of this book.

Copyright 2012 Keith E. Ouellette
Kouell Publishing

Acknowledgements

I would like to acknowledge several sources of the data used in this book. Specifically:

A. John Mauldin, "Thoughts from the Frontline," a Weekly Investment and Economic newsletter;

B. Doug Short, Advisor Perspectives;

C. Global Economic Intersection;

D. FRED - Federal Reserve Economic Database from the Federal Reserve Bank of St. Louis;

E. AmosWeb.com - the Economic encyclopedia;

F. StreetTalkLive.com

G. The Heritage Foundation

H. FactCheck.org

Introduction

I conceived the idea for this book during the Republican debates and their attacks on President Obama's Democratic Party in mid-2012. It was a split Congress with Democrats controlling the Senate and Republicans controlling the House. The Tea Party movement against government spending swung the interim elections in 2010 in the Republicans favor. After Democrats passed the Affordable Health Care Law prior to the 2010 interim elections, this period of U.S. Political History became classic "right-wing versus left-wing" warfare and Congress found itself in gridlock.

The U.S. was indeed in a deep recession for 18 months during 2008/2009, mainly caused by the collapse of the real estate bubble and financial institutions "holding the bag" of unpaid mortgages. The "ripple effect" of loose lending standards contributed to runaway housing values at the turn of the new millennium. After the loss of 30-40% of the equity in their homes, some consumers stopped spending, paying their mortgages and walked away from their debt obligations. We can add greed to the mix as one of the underlying causes of failed policies in our financial system.

Who was watching the U. S. bank account? . . . the Federal Reserve, Security Exchange Commission or Congress? The answer is simply:

√ **None of the Above**

While we were all watching and supporting the changes made in the security of our country after the 2001 Terrorist attacks, everything else took a back seat for almost a decade during the Bush Administration. The wars in Afghanistan and Iraq contributed to the rising debt of the U.S. For 10 years, we were obsessed with defeating Saddam Hussein, Osama Bin Laden, the Taliban and Al Qaida.

It is an oxymoron that Republicans loosened the purse strings to fund the effort with Democratic support to protect our borders. Normally, we would see the major political parties keep each other in balance. So, the U.S. experienced out of control government spending for 8 years, along with the "free markets" padding their own bank accounts without any oversight or concern for their effect on the future economy. The result was the largest "collapse" of several industries, including residential construction, manufacturing and financial institutions holding worthless mortgage-backed securities in the biggest legal scam of the 21st Century to date.

THE U.S. ECONOMY EXPOSED – Debt Crisis!

The Obama Administration had no chance whatsoever to ebb the tide in the free fall towards the deepest recession since The Great Depression of 1929. After the 2008 election, the Democrats saw their chance to pass a massive health care reform package, much to the demise of the U. S. economy. It was good timing for the Democrats to get health care through Congress, but bad timing for the economy. Although most of the changes would not take effect until 2013-2014, the damage to the credibility of the Democratic Party and our economy could not be stopped.

The rise of the new Tea Party movement, whose right-wing policies promote massive cuts in government spending, would destroy the Democrats in the mid-term elections of 2010 and create a split Congress, which contributed to the "gridlock" for the next 2 years of the Obama Administration.

With the 2012 re-election of Obama, I found it somewhat humorous that the Republicans blamed the Administration for its failed policies. But, it has been truly Republican party policies that created the deepest recession since 1929, including allowing the free market to wheel and deal, implementing major tax cuts, funding the war on terror, and cutting government spending in areas where we needed the funding most.

THE U.S. ECONOMY EXPOSED – Debt Crisis!

This book takes a look at the history of recessions and the political party in power just prior to the downturns in the economy. Since World War II, the following chart illustrates who controlled Congress and the Presidency before and after each recession.

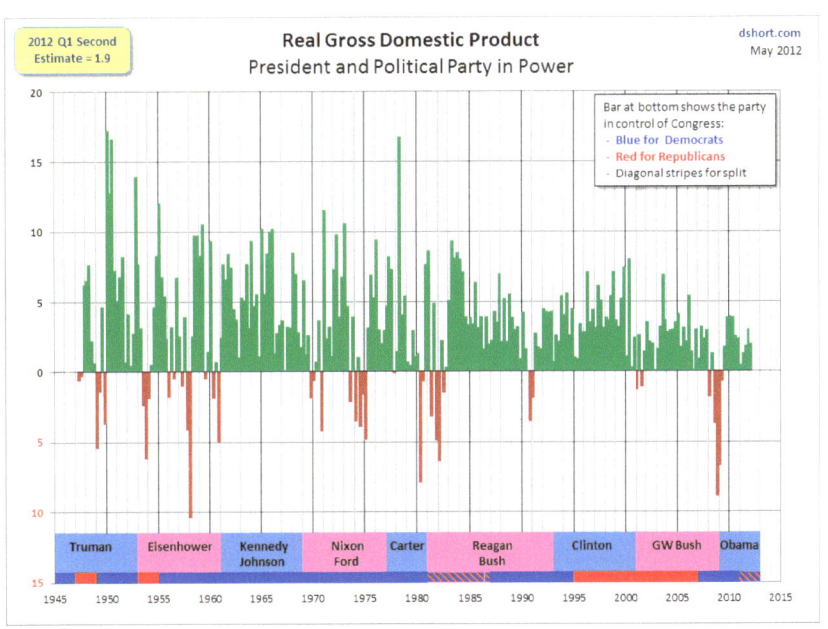

One could argue that the increase in government spending on Wars got us out of or delayed the recessions, specifically World War II in the 1940s, the Korean and Vietnam wars in the 1950s and 1960s, and the Afghanistan/Iraq wars in the 2000s. The longest periods of prosperity in the U.S. were under the Reagan/Bush era in the 1980s and the Clinton era in the 1990s.

THE U.S. ECONOMY EXPOSED – Debt Crisis!

Take a look at Debt-to-GDP ratio during the war years. World War II and the Afghanistan/Iraq Wars show a sudden spurt in the Debt/GDP ratio. Obviously, the financial bail-out exacerbated the problem during the Great Recession. With a Split-Congress, it is forecasted that Government spending will get back to normal levels.

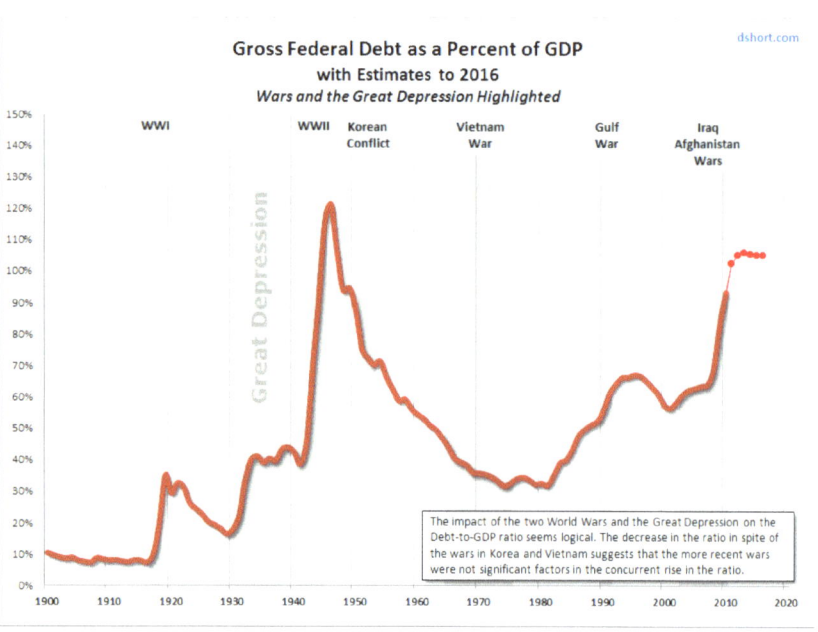

Notice the drop in Debt/GDP ratio in the 1990s. This occurred during the Clinton years with the Balanced Budget Amendment. The U.S. needs to go there again whether through tax increases, cuts in spending or a combination of both. In my opinion, Congress will have to make both choices.

THE U.S. ECONOMY EXPOSED – Debt Crisis!

The Oil Embargo of the 1970s caused the highest period of inflation, after a severe recession in the mid-1970s, which derailed the Carter Administration without a chance for survival. The Democratic Congress could not survive 17% inflation and high interest rates in the 1980 election.

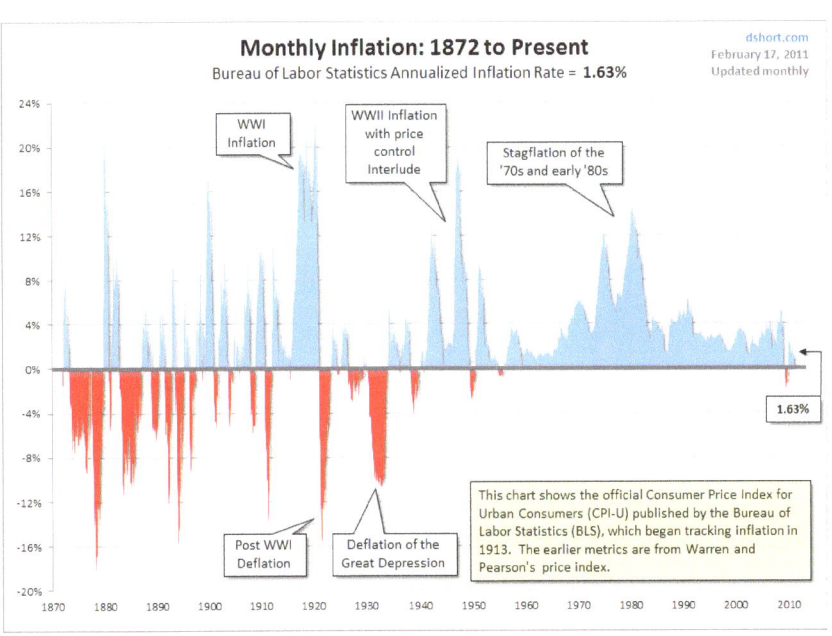

Enter Reagan and his supply-side economics in the 1980s, kept somewhat in check by a split Congress. Inflation has been under control ever since, possibly until now. Will the U.S. experience the return of runaway inflation? A lot of people seem to think so, which is why they have been investing in gold and other precious metals. In any event, investment in our stock and bond markets have been curtailed and have fluctuated wildly over the last 2-3 years.

We are a nation in disarray and some don't know what to do with their money in this economic environment, while the majority of us struggle to make ends meet. Our focus here is to look at what Congressional decisions were made before and after recessions, and their resulting impact on GDP growth in the U.S. economy. I want to illustrate to you that what matters most to an improved economy is:

1) the Party controlling Congress and
2) the Administration in power of the Presidency.

The Party in control of both Houses and the Presidency swings far to the Left or to the Right, causing imbalance in the economy. History shows that Balance and Prosperity are achieved when the pendulum swings towards the middle.

Can we learn from past mistakes? Or, do we have a filibuster of choices to make over the next decade. I believe it will take that long for us to get out of our Debt situation, both from an individual consumer and U.S. Economic standpoint. We have let the "Free Markets" run wild for too long. It is time to put the train back on the right track to prosperity.

Chapter 1 – A Fair Comparison?

"It ain't over until its over"
. . . Yogi Berra

JOBS: It would be impossible to compare GDP spending levels during the 15-year recovery period after the 1929 Depression and our current 3-year recovery period after the 2008/2009 recession. Will it take another 10-12 years to get the U.S. back to 4-5% GDP Growth? Some say, yes, especially since the U.S. Debt levels are on their way to exceeding 100% of GDP as it did back then.

The biggest difference between now and then is the unemployment level, 25-30% in the 1930s as compared to 8-10% in 2010-12. Is the government "toying" with these numbers? Yes, I believe they are to prevent a run on the banks and the destruction of our financial system. But let's consider the make-up of the current work-force now versus then. Today, we have work-at-home businesses, an aging population, use of Temporary Labor by small business to avoid paying benefits, and an Information society with data accessible literally at your fingertips. Based on these factors alone, the U.S. should experience an easier recovery now than they did in the 1930s.

What type of jobs will be created? An increase in a part-time workforce? Certainly, there will be some tough decisions to make in the next decade with Baby Boomers expecting to retire in droves, or will they?

This chart illustrates the loss of jobs, at least those the government is counting, during the Great Recession:

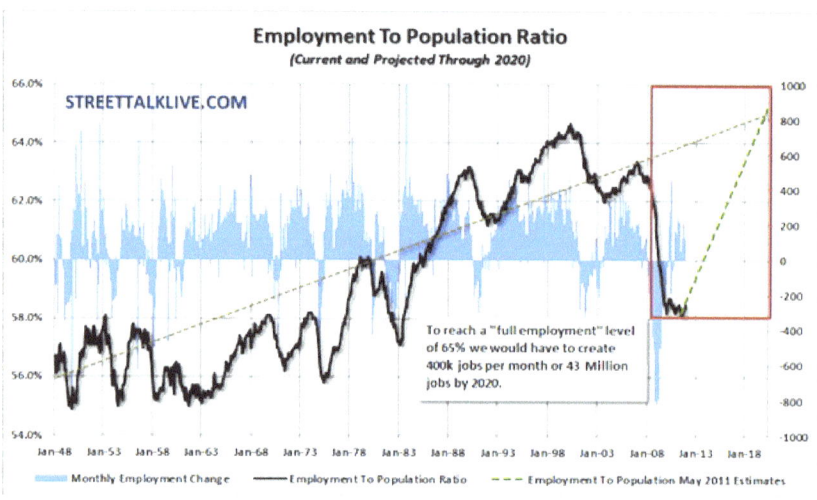

We clearly have a long way to go to reach full employment even without knowing how many people really need to work, but have stopped looking for jobs. The Baby Boomers are getting ready to retire, but I truly believe that they have to come up with a way to supplement their income in "The New Retirement" years. Innovation is key in creating these new opportunities.

THE U.S. ECONOMY EXPOSED – Debt Crisis!

SOCIAL PROGRAMS: It is also impossible to compare the GDP spending levels between the 2 periods because our social programs did not exist until 10 years after the Depression. Was this the lost decade back then, similar to our lost decade during the War on Terror? We also experienced the "Roaring 80s and 90s" just 10 years prior to The Great Recession, similar to the "Roaring 20s" just prior to The Great Depression. Coincidence or will history repeat itself? I believe that the lost decade "spent" in the War on Terror delayed a more normal recovery period, extended the business cycle, increased our Debt to mid-1940 levels, and created this catastrophic hole. The Feds were not minding the store.

The New Deal of the 1930s and 1940s introduced Social Security in 1935, while Medicare/Medicaid programs were not fully in place until the mid-1960s. So, it would be an unfair comparison of U.S. GDP Spending habits between those periods. However, you could draw a link from the Roosevelt's New Deal to Obama's Health Care Reform as social spending comparisons. We have not had an opportunity to play out the Health Care Reform cards yet. There is no question in my mind that we will have to reform all of our social programs and tax laws due to the aging population. You can expect another "New Deal" for the next decade.

DEBT to GDP RATIO: The intriguing events in the years after World War II saw the Debt/GDP ratio fall 60 points to a more sustainable level, even after implementing Medicare/Medicaid programs in the the mid-1960s. Republicans blame the Obama and the Democrats for the increase in Government spending. While I agree that Government Spending increased due to the financial bailouts and Federal Reserve policy on Quantitative Easing, we most certainly would have been in a deep depression, not recession, the 2nd of its kind in our history, if the government did not step in to bail out the economy.

Clearly, we have had a slowdown in GDP due to lower **C**onsumer Spending, which accounts for 70% of the GDP equation, **C+I+G+(E-M)**. Private **I**nvestment has also dropped by 10%. If "**C**" (Consumption) dropped by 10% and "**I**" (Investment) dropped by 10% during The Great Recession, then what had to happen? The "**G**" (Government Spending) had to increase dramatically to make up the some of the difference. The effect of **E**xports minus i**M**ports is negligible, but has helped the U.S. keep out of a double dip recession territory during the slow recovery period in 2012. There are more moving parts to the internal workings of the economy, but it they are outside the scope of the book. I am trying to keep this as simple as possible here for most of you.

THE U.S. ECONOMY EXPOSED – Debt Crisis!

Here is an illustration of what occurred between the 2 periods.

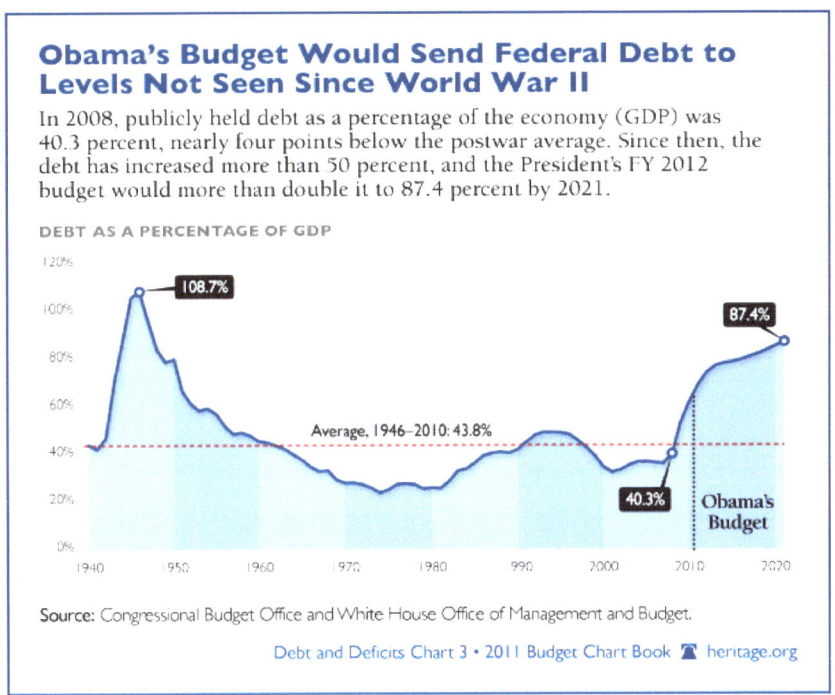

The sudden increase in the Debt/GDP ratio after 1940, clearly is the direct result of funding "The New Deal" and World War II. We also see the sudden increase in the Debt/GDP ratio during the GW Bush years before the 2008 election. Budgets are set for 1-2 years before a new Administration can have any impact on economic policy. Obama inherited Republican ideologies, but the recession put his own policies on the back-burner during the downturn, except for some semblance of a new health care reform system, a poor attempt at best.

THE U.S. ECONOMY EXPOSED – Debt Crisis!

In light of the massive improvement in the Debt/GDP ratio shortly after World War II, can we duplicate it in the coming years? Clearly, it will take some time and tough decisions by Congress to get us out of this mess. It took us 15 years to move from 108% Debt/GDP ratio in 1946 to 40% in 1960. During that time, the U.S. experienced 2 recessions under Truman and 3 recessions under Eisenhower, so neither party is recession-proof.

Some economists say that we are in a Secular Bear Market. These periods of history show that the stock market fluctuates wildly, but settle back to the same level at its end as it was in the beginning. Here is an interesting table shared tongue in cheek by John Mauldin in his "Frontline" newsletter.

Period	Dow Begin of Period	Dow End of Period	Type of Market
1929 - 1947	380	220	Lean Cycle-Bear
1947 - 1965	220	900	Fat Cycle-Bull
1965 - 1982	900	900	Lean Cycle-Bear
1982 - 2000	900	11,500	Fat Cycle-Bull
2000 - 2018	11,500	????	Lean Cycle-Bear

Cycles are approximately 18 years long.

Will history repeat itself during the current recovery period over the next 6 years? We are 2/3 of the way through the Secular Bear Cycle before the next Bull market and we are stuck around a 12-13,000 point Dow as of the date of this writing. Coincidence?

Only time will tell and as Yogi Berra put it so eloquently,

"It ain't over until it's over"

Chapter 2 – The New Deal

"The only thing we have to fear is fear itself"
. . . Franklin D. Roosevelt

Does Obama have the **influence** to get the job done with Congress? It took Franklin D. Roosevelt from 1933 to 1945 to implement the New Deal and overhaul our entire banking system, creating the highest Debt/GDP ratio at 108%. Was it the New Deal that got us out of the Depression, or was it World War II and the industrial revolution? Let's take a look at the tax brackets since 1900 and how the massive tax cuts during the Reagan/Bush era reduced our ability to balance the budget.

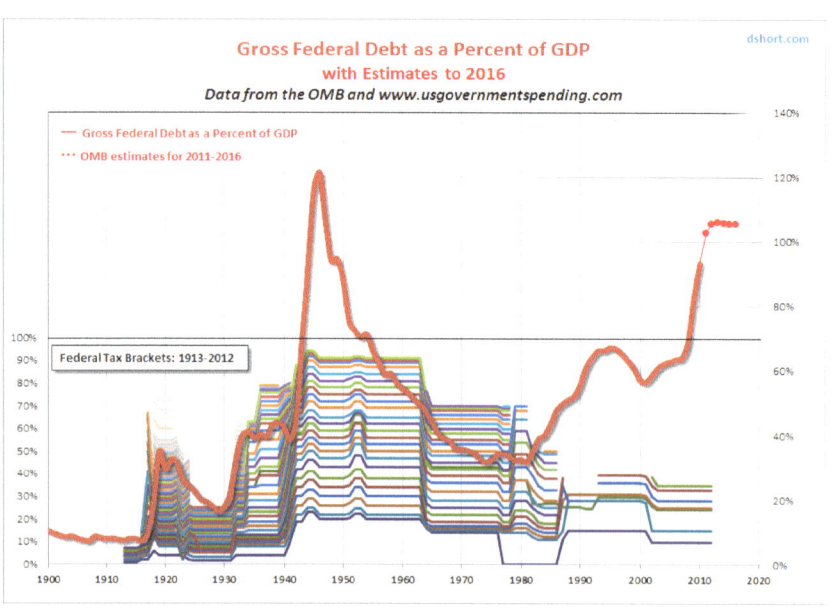

THE U.S. ECONOMY EXPOSED – Debt Crisis!

The Republicans implemented the largest series of tax cuts in history to stimulate the economy and one of the longest periods of prosperity. However, it also caused the Debt/GDP ratio to skyrocket as it did during the World War II era. We do not have much room to play with anymore, although the Republicans and the new Tea Party are still calling for even more tax cuts. Where will the Government get the funds to maintain current spending levels, let alone increase them to pay for The Affordable Care Act, or most commonly known as ObamaCare?

Despite propaganda surrounding government spending, the U.S. has consistently been hovering around 20% of GDP. Here is a breakdown in the major components of GDP over the last 38 years (the dark blue line is Government Spending):

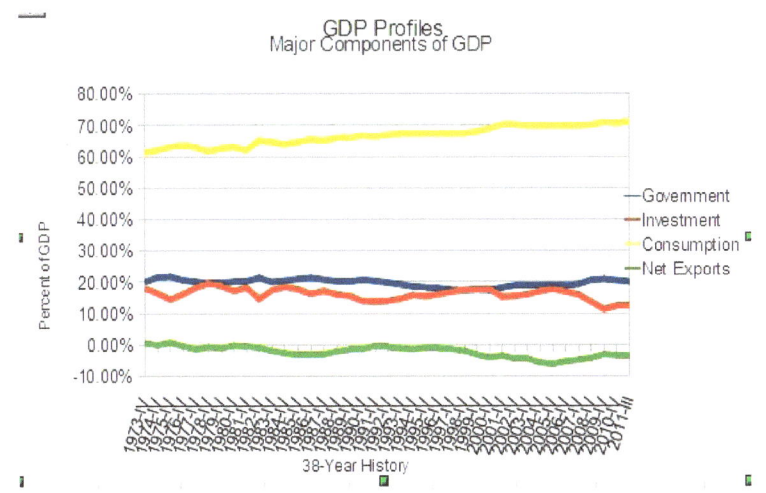

THE U.S. ECONOMY EXPOSED – Debt Crisis!

As you can see, the percentage fell below 20% during the Clinton years, which was one of the longest periods of prosperity in the U.S. How was this accomplished you might ask? . . . through a Balanced Budget Amendment, the smartest decision made by Congress in recent history. Unfortunately, we are far from a balanced budget with limited prospects of achieving it in the near future.

Clearly, the 20-year period, 1980-2000, was the longest period of prosperity since the Depression years with one small recession in 1990-1991. Both parties were in political power during this time period and neither party can take all the credit. So, what gives and why can't we go back to the good old times? Here are two reasons:

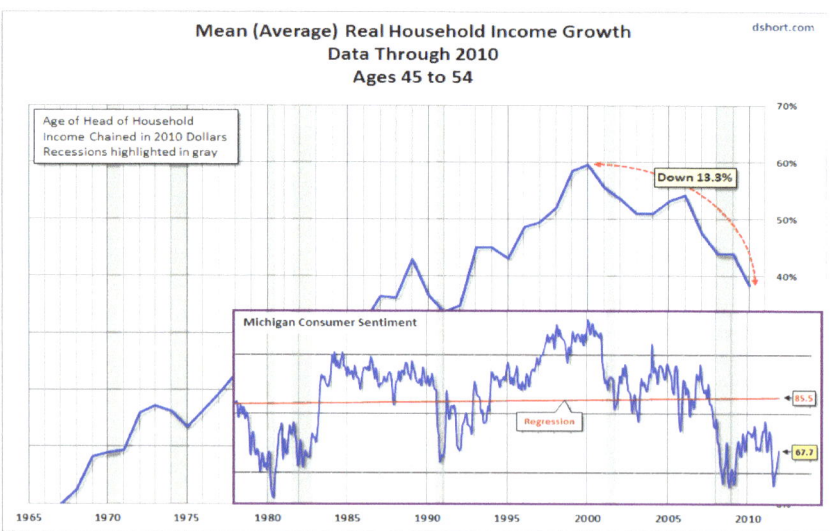

THE U.S. ECONOMY EXPOSED – Debt Crisis!

Not only have consumers lost their spending power, but their confidence in the U.S. economy has dropped to all-time lows. Will consumers spend itself out of recession territory? I do not believe it will anytime soon! Here is the breakdown of financial wealth distribution in the U.S.

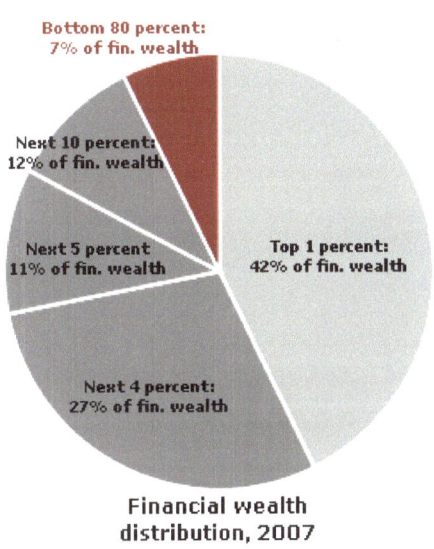

Financial wealth distribution, 2007

The top 10% owns 80% of the wealth in the U.S. but do not consume as much as the bottom 80% of our people. So, we as a nation are in serious financial trouble. Consumption, representing 70% of GDP, and Government, representing 20% of GDP, are not expected to grow the economy in the short term.

Neither will major increases in Exports significantly exceed Imports to have much of an impact on GDP. So, what will?

The only possible hope for the short-term appears to be Private Investment! Since 1974, Investment has dropped 6 points from a high of 18% of GDP to 12%. From where will this increase come. Let's first take a look at Corporate Profits.

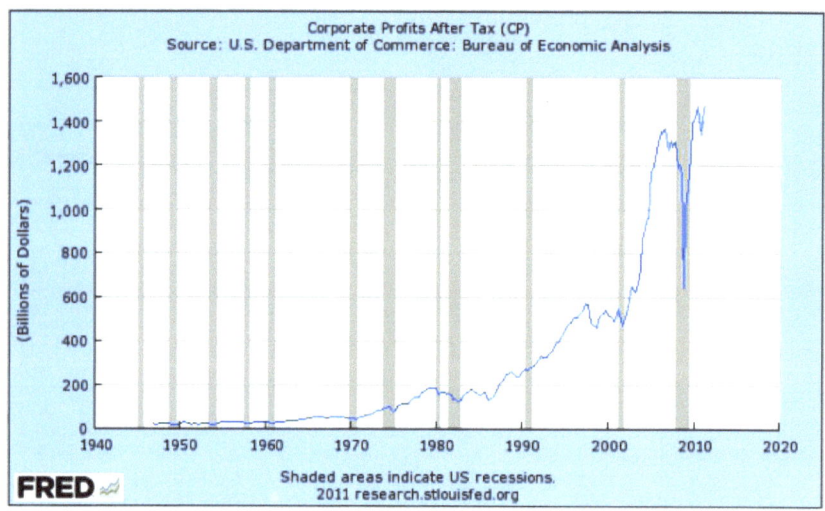

Will Corporate America invest in the growth of the New Economy? Although corporate profits have been exceeding all-time highs over the last few years, companies have not been re-investing their profits into the economy. They too have been hoarding excess cash and saving it for a rainy day, similar to what banks are doing with the Feds' bailout funds! The challenge for the Federal Reserve and the Administration will be to develop programs for the banks and business to use their excess cash reserves. Demand for goods and services must increase before businesses will be begin hiring again and paying higher wages for value-added or improved services.

It is time for New Deal II! Who is going to lead us out of this mess? I don't see much happening with GDP Growth barring another War, but the U.S. Congress can work on a New Deal to help stimulate the economy. It is clear from this chart that the U.S. needs to invest in the economy to grow it.

GDP COMPONENTS	1974 - 1975	2010 - 2011
CONSUMPTION	61%	71%
GOVERNMENT	20%	20%
INVESTMENT	18%	12%
EXPORTS - IMPORTS	1%	(3%)

We need to recover the 6 points lost in Investment since the mid-1970s and somehow stimulate Exports before consumer and business confidence can be restored. It would be difficult to grow the economy through Investment alone. The European recession of 2012 will also reduce 1) the amount of exports from the U.S. and 2) Corporate Profits, both of which will negatively impact GDP growth in the short-term. As a result, a full recovery will take years for us to get back to normal growth levels. Will the next 6 years be enough time to start the next Bull Market?

With the New Deal, Consumption would follow after companies make the investment in people, increasing wages and disposable income. This is our long-term solution since we need time to gain confidence back in our Government! After a period of stimulating the Economy under the **New Deal** (whatever it may be), Government spending will be controlled and the Budget balanced.

This is all good in theory, but the timing and implementation of the necessary decisions is critical. We require a Bi-Partisan Congress to pass the necessary laws to get us through it.

THE U.S. ECONOMY EXPOSED – Debt Crisis!

In the next Chapter, we take a closer look at the comparisons between The Great Depression and The Great Recession before, during and after these major downturns in our economy. What can we expect to happen in the short-term? Can we anticipate and forecast the future based on what happened in the past? Will the Split Congress be able to lead us through the recovery and help the majority of us achieve prosperity?

Chapter 3 - A Closer Look!

"Always Invest for the Long-Term!"
Warren Buffett

The U.S. must take heed to these words spoken by the greatest investor of all-time, Warren Buffett. Unfortunately, recent decisions made by Congress are clearly for the short-term due to our biennial election system. Every elected official is worried about losing their job and party seats, rather than making the necessary choices to do the right thing over time. Congress continues to delay hard decisions for another time, exacerbating the critical problems which need to be addressed.

Specifically, the Social Security, Medicare & Medicaid systems need an overhaul after well over 50-60 years in place. They were developed during a time when Baby Boomers were expected to contribute to the programs for 50-60 years. Now that Boomers are expected to retire in droves and the labor force is expected to shrink, the Social Programs will become insolvent for years to come unless the systems are overhauled. Combined with ObamaCare, the U.S. cannot sustain the costs of these programs without corresponding reductions in other areas or tax increases to help pay for them.

THE U.S. ECONOMY EXPOSED – Debt Crisis!

We must think about a long-term solution and invest in America through a combination of spending cuts and tax increases. Population trends, workforce solutions, and improved efficiencies to produce more goods and services on a per capita basis must be considered over another 50-60 year period, preferably a 75-80 year cycle. Consider this . . . The Great Depression in 1929 and The Great Recession in 2009 spanned 80 years. The similarities between the 2 periods are uncanny.

The Inflationary Periods:

1929 – 1933	2007 – 2008
Federal Reserve doubles its holdings of government securities	Feds more than doubles assets on its balance sheet; banks build up excess reserves; and effect on money supply is minimal
Federal Reserve lowers the rediscount rate from 6% to 2%; money supply is stagnant	Feds lower the federal funds rate from 5.25% in Sep 2006 to 1% by Oct 2008
Congress approves the expenditure of a giant $915 million public works program and subsidizes many industries	Feds inject billions to bail-out financial institutions to battle the problems that banks have with bad investments
Government expenses rise from 14.3% of Gross Private Product (GPP) in 1929 to 18.2% in 1930 to 24% in 1931	*Still at 22-24% of GDP, but the Split Congress is preventing accelerated Government Spending after the excessive financial bail-outs*

The underlying cause of these two events was GREED and CORRUPTION. What did the Feds do to stimulate the economy?

The Great Depression and The Great Recession:

1921-1929	2001-2007
A sharp recession occurs during 1920	A sharp recession occurs in the year 2001
The 1920s boom is kicked off: the Feds inflate money supply via credit expansion	The Feds inflate the money supply via credit expansion in 2001 - 2006
The Dow Jones Industrial Average soars from 63.90 in 1921 to 381.17 in Oct 1929	The Dow Jones Industrial Avg surges from 7528 in Sept 2002 to 14093 in Oct 2007
A liquidation of unsound investments is kicked off by the crash of Oct 1929	Stock market liquidation is kicked off with the crash of Oct 2007

Whatever we do, decisions must be made for the long-term. No more bandaids, please! Take this opportunity to rid the economy of Medicare/Medicaid and Social Security fraud, and implement a healthcare system that will not allow greed and corruption to take hold.

In the next Chapter, we take a look at the 12-year recovery period after The Great Depression led by FDR and his New Deal.

Chapter 4 - New Deal II?

*"I pledge you, I pledge myself, to
a new deal for the American people."*
Franklin D. Roosevelt

What was this New Deal that Roosevelt implemented during his 12-year reign as President from 1933 to 1945? The New Deal was a variety of programs designed to produce <u>relief</u> (government jobs for the unemployed), <u>recovery</u> (economic growth), and <u>reform</u> (through regulation of Wall Street, banks and transportation).

The economy improved rapidly from 1933 to 1937, but then relapsed into a deep recession again. Along with several smaller programs, major surviving programs include the Federal Deposit Insurance Corporation, which was created in 1933, and Social Security, which Congress passed in 1935.

As World War II loomed after 1938, with the Japanese invasion of China and the aggressions of Nazi Germany, Roosevelt gave strong diplomatic and financial support to China and the United Kingdom, while remaining officially neutral. His goal was to make America the "Arsenal of Democracy" which would supply munitions to the Allies. With very strong national support, he made war on Japan and Germany after the Japanese attack on Pearl Harbor on December 7, 1941 and supervised the mobilization of the U.S. economy to support the Allied war effort, which gave rise to its ultimate recovery.

If history repeats itself again, the U.S. will enter into another Recession after a short recovery period. What will get us out of this one? Another World War? It may be inevitable, but I don't want to make this prediction at this juncture!

We are in the period 80 years after Roosevelt took office in 1933. Now that Obama has won a 2nd term, will the Republican-controlled House become more receptive towards compromise with the Administration? The bottom line is that we have to find solutions to reduce our debt. All that I know for sure is that the Administration must encourage bi-partisanship with Congress and lead the U.S. to prosperity, just as Reagan did in the 1980s. Republicans continue to call for tax cuts. However, we are at a point in our history with the lowest personal tax rates, thanks to the Reagan/Bush years and the GW Bush tax cuts.

Circumstances are different this time. That is why I am calling this period in history "New Deal II." GDP Growth is not going to be stimulated by tax cuts alone. We need more tax incentive programs for small business to stimulate Investment!

Also, major tax reform is necessary . . . whether the U.S. Congress passes a flat income tax system, or we implement a Value-Added Tax (VAT) on luxury items, mostly imposed on the rich, not mainstream America. It should be noted here that Obama wants to impose higher income tax rates to help pay for the Affordable Care Act, but it is highly unlikely major tax increases will get through Congress.

People should be aware that most universal health care systems were implemented in the period following the Second World War as a process of deliberate health care reform, intended to make health care available to all, in the spirit of Article 25 of the Universal Declaration of Human Rights of 1948, signed by every country doing so. The US <u>did not ratify</u> the social and economic rights sections, including Article 25's right to health. So, here we are, the only civilized country in the world without universal health care since World War II, trying to implement it now in the midst of the 2nd highest Debt-to-GDP ratio in our short history.

Because the Affordable Care Act is now embedded into law and supported by the Supreme Court decision that the health insurance mandate is constitutional, the new Administration will have no choice but to work within the boundaries imposed on it.

New Deal II requires major tax and healthcare reform to pay for multiple program changes, including Social Security, Medicare/Medicaid and reduce U.S. Debt over the next 10-15 years down to manageable levels.

Before we can come up with solutions to fix the economy, we must take a closer look at the components of GDP and determine what will stimulate economic growth. We have already ruled out Consumption, Government Spending, and Exports to help us in the short-term. So, we must focus on Private Investment, which we will cover in the next Chapter.

Chapter 5 - Private Investment

"Eliminating the Death Tax will continue to restore consumer confidence, spur capital investment, and create new jobs which are critical components of economic growth, particularly within the small business community"

Howard Coble

This quote made by the U.S. Representative from North Carolina, Howard Coble, is one of many tax cut proposals being made by the Republican Party to stimulate Gross Private Investment in the economy. I don't understand how a personal tax would stimulate business investment, especially since small business stimulates capital investment and new jobs. But, let's take a look at the components of Gross Private Domestic Investment (GDPI) to see if Coble's statement makes any sense.

The components of GDPI includes:

1. all final purchases of machinery, equipment, and tools by businesses
2. all construction (including factories, stores, etc. AND residential construction)
3. changes in inventories (positive and negative)
4. does NOT include stocks, bonds., etc., (financial investments)

This is worth repeating . . . _GPDI does not include financial investments._ I really wonder how many of the Top 5% of the Wealthy really put their excess cash into business as a capital investment? We need to take a closer look at the Investment component of GDP based on excerpts taken from AmosWeb.com.

B. Two Investment Categories

Gross private domestic investment is officially separated into two categories: 1) fixed investment and 2) changes in private inventories. This is where all of the business activity in the economy takes place. For now, I will ignore the activity that takes place within each business i.e. The exchange of labor for wages, since it will complicate matters and crosses into the other components of GDP.

Fixed investment is the category that includes the capital goods that best reflects what most people believe is capital investment made in structures and durable goods. For 2-3 years now, the auto industry has propped up our economy and is the light that is guiding us to recovery. These investments are generally about 95 percent of GPDI. This category includes factories, machinery, tools, and buildings. It is not stocks and bonds! More specifically, fixed investment is divided into two major subcategories: a) _nonresidential and b) residential._

The *nonresidential* category, once again, typifies what most people think of as business investment. Coming in at approximately 70 percent of gross private domestic investment, this subcategory includes structures (buildings, pipelines, oil wells) and producers' durable equipment (computers, machinery, vehicles). Structures are about 25% of nonresidential fixed investment and producers' durable equipment is about 75%.

The *residential* category primarily includes houses and apartments, and comes in at around 30 percent of both fixed investment and gross private domestic investment. Like nonresidential fixed investment, residential fixed investment is divided into structures and producers' durable equipment. Structures are separated into single family (houses) and multifamily (apartments). They can be owned by either a business or an individual. In other words, the production of an owner-occupied house is included as gross private domestic investment. This is the only notable purchase made by the household sector that is not included as a personal consumption expenditure. Structures are about 98 percent of this residential category and producers' durable equipment is the remaining 2 percent.

B. Changes in Inventory

Change in private inventories is investment by the business sector in finished products, intermediate goods, raw materials that businesses keep on hand to use in production. Inventories also include final goods that have been produced but remain unsold. These are considered investment because businesses need inventories to smooth the flow of production and sales.

Changes in private inventories tend to be about 3 to 5 percent of gross private domestic investment. But while small, they are a highly volatile component. The reason is the inventories act as a buffer between aggregate expenditures and aggregate production. If aggregate expenditures exceed aggregate production, then private business inventories fall. If aggregate production exceeds aggregate expenditures, then private inventories rise. This volatility is an indicator of business-cycle instability.

Two categories of private inventory changes are included: farm and non-farm. Non-Farm is further separated into the subcategories of manufacturing, wholesale trade, and retail trade, with manufacturing usually the largest of the three. The change in inventory has minimal impact on GDP.

THE U.S. ECONOMY EXPOSED – Debt Crisis!

So why has Private Investment dropped by 33%, or 6 points from 18% to 12% of Total GDP since 1974? Let's take a look at the numbers visually.

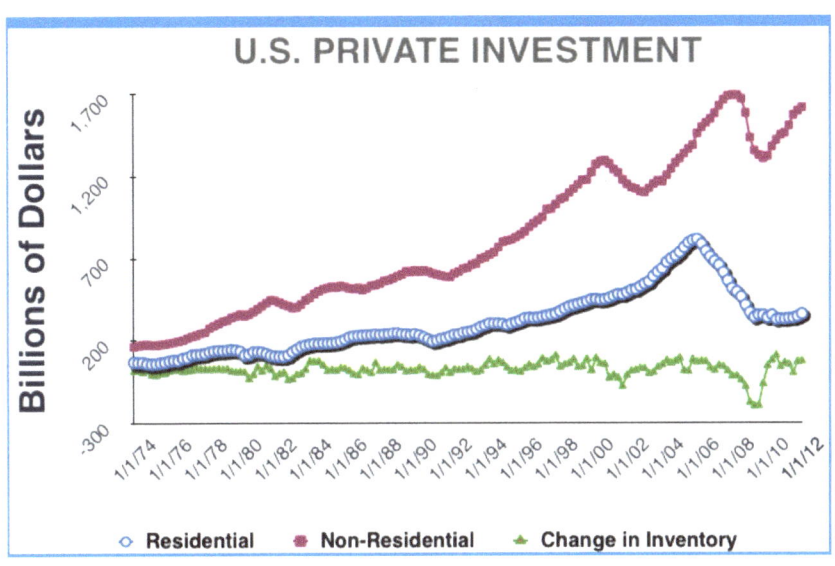

Clearly, investment of capital in the residential segment took a major downturn with the collapse of the real estate bubble. The problem over the last few years is that it has "flatlined." Although residential investment only represents 30% of this major component of GDP, the crash has had a significant impact on our current slow growth economy. The volatility of Business activity in the Non-Residential category over the last few years has contributed to the rise and fall of the stock market, allowing wealth to increase only for the rich and famous.

Corporate profits have reached all-time highs before and after (in 2012) The Great Recession. So, why hasn't this business activity had more of an impact on GDP growth? Unfortunately, Investment only accounts for 10% of GDP. A 10% growth rate in corporate profits would affect GDP by less than 1%. For argument's sake, tax reductions theoretically would stimulate growth in jobs, employee income and consumption. So far, that has not happened during this recovery period.

The Republicans continue to believe that by lowering business taxes, this action alone will stimulate job growth and consumer spending. It clearly will not! We have already covered that aspect in an earlier chapter. The problem is that banks, businesses and consumers are all hoarding their cash, or paying down debts. Although fiscally-responsible, debt payoff does nothing to stimulate the economy, since it is paying for past services or goods rendered.

We should now take a look specifically at Corporate Profits and how it compares to the overall trend of Non-Residential component of Investment. It does have the same double dip trend in growth, which speaks highly to its contribution to the Investment portion of the economy.

THE U.S. ECONOMY EXPOSED – Debt Crisis!

Here is a graphical depiction of Corporate Profits.

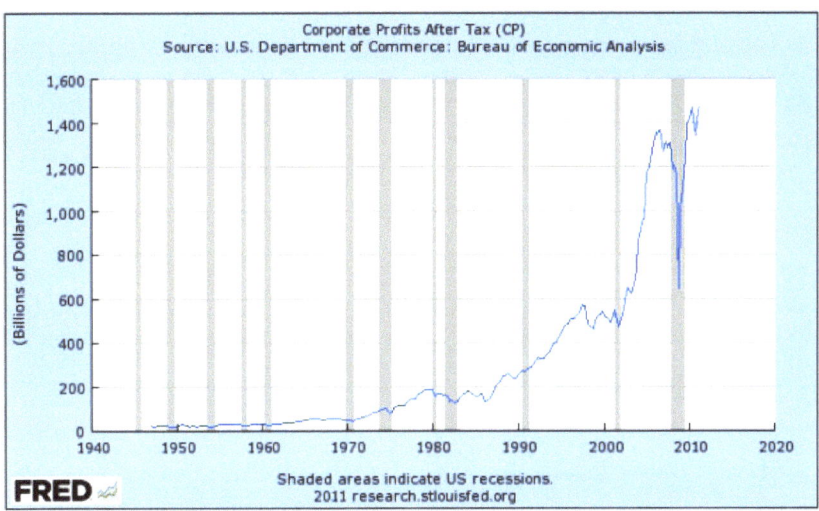

After 2002, Corporate Profits soared to the highest levels ever achieved in history, more than doubling their profits in 3-5 years. By 2006, the Business Cycle turned and signaled the coming downturn in the economy. Greed and corruption took hold, while the U.S. Government focused on the War on Terror. It wasn't until the collapse of real estate values and the financial markets in 2007 that it got some attention in Congress. By then, it was too late to do much of anything. Hence, the U.S. moved into period of the lost decade.

Despite record Corporate Profits, the economy has still not made much of an attempt in its recovery. So what will?

THE U.S. ECONOMY EXPOSED – Debt Crisis!

The Final Chapter
"For Now . . ."

What will stimulate this economy? . . . Another round of Quantitative Easing by the Feds? No, I don't believe that would do much of anything! Cash reserves are aplenty in the current economy, hoarded by the wealthiest individuals, banks and businesses. Take a look at the Excess Cash Reserves.

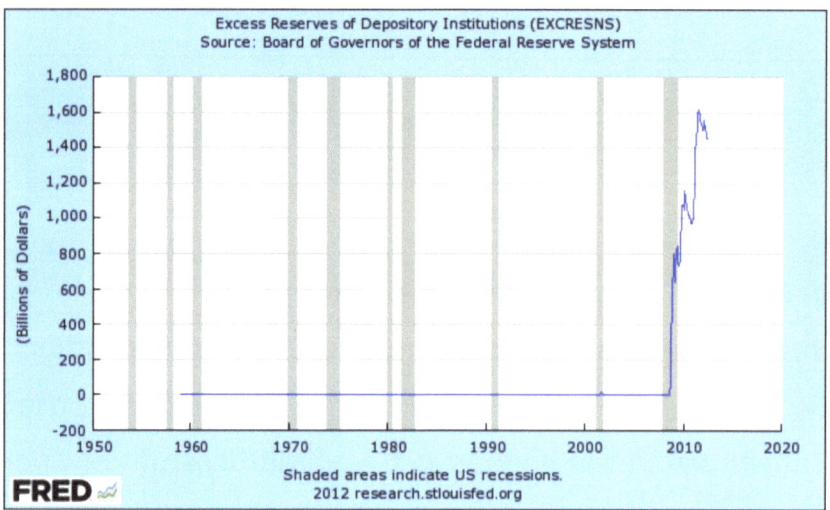

Banks have tightened their credit standards, at least 1/3 of Americans have poor credit to qualify for loans, disposable income has fallen dramatically for consumers and businesses refuse to invest in new hirings due to low demand. Coupled with the pressure to reduce Government Spending, the economic outlook does not look good over the next 5-6 years, if nothing is done to stimulate the movement of cash into the economy.

The best indicators to watch are Consumer Confidence and Small Business Optimism that will signal improvement in the overall economy. Let's take a look at the most recent consumer confidence level.

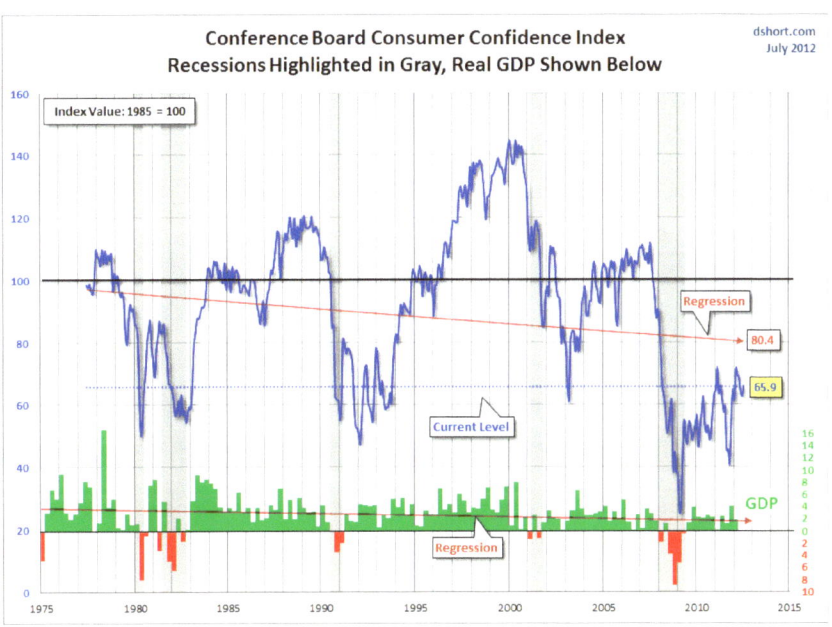

Consumer confidence is significantly lower than normal levels of the last 40 years, but this index is extremely volatile. Given the fact that the stock market has been extremely volatile during the slow recovery, Business Optimism has followed suit. We have a long way to go before mainstream America will loosen their purse strings to start spending again. This is clearly evident even with the Feds holding down interest rates close to zero and long-term mortgage rates significantly under 5%.

The growth in Consumer Spending and Residential Investment is just not there yet, and the trend in both indexes converge on each other, as illustrated in the National Federation of Independent Business (NFIB) Business Optimism index below.

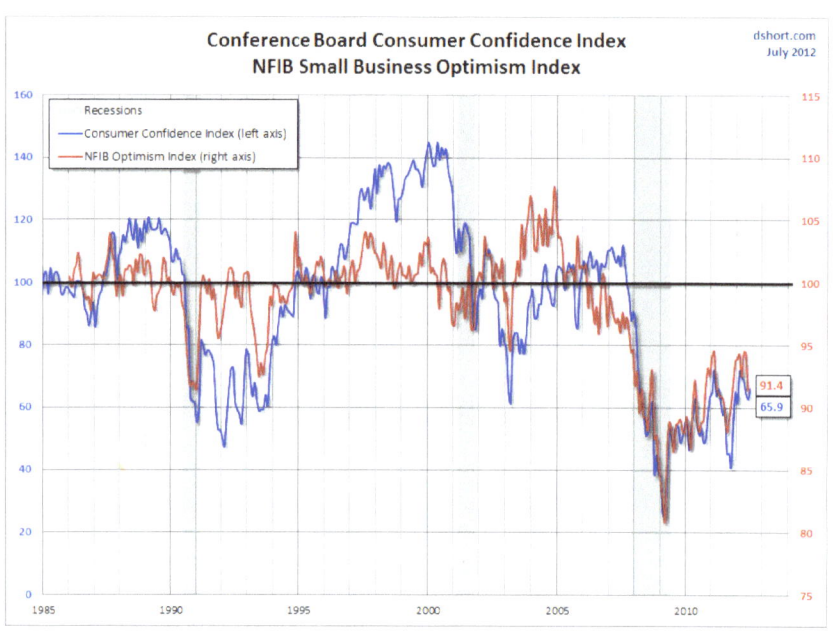

As stated by Doug Short in his Advisor Perspectives blog, "With the latest NFIB data, we see that the mood of small businesses is again matching the decline seen in the recent consumer confidence updates." The fall in corporate profits during the last 2 quarters, clearly caused small business optimism to wane even more. So, what is next for the current economy during the last half of 2012? The conclusion to the NFIB's commentary on the current trend in the economy is this:

"The economy definitely slowed mid-year, not a huge recession threat but slower than earlier in the year. Job growth will be far short of that needed to reduce the unemployment rate unless lots of unemployed leave the labor force. NFIB members didn't add a lot of jobs and don't plan to in the coming months. Capital spending and inventory investment also weakened. Expectations for improvements in sales and business conditions faded, so no reason to hire additional workers or buy new inventory. Political uncertainty remained historically high as the reason why the current period is not a good time to expand. All in all, this month's survey was a real economic downer."

We need a New Deal put in place that will encourage innovation to stimulate both consumer spending and business investment. Congress also needs to take a long hard look at Tax Reform and revamping all social programs, including Social Security, Medicare and Medicaid. Our objective should be to eliminate fraud and corruption, which accounts for an estimated $100 Billion by some experts, or 5-10% of the total cost of healthcare in the U.S.

While the cost of fraud is just a drop in the bucket for paying the incremental cost of The Affordable Care Act, most European countries have a Value-Added Tax (VAT) to help pay for their national healthcare systems. This is a tax on luxury items, and not basic need purchases made by the majority of the people. Rather than just increase the tax rates of the wealthy, this would be a fair and more equitable approach than what Obama is promoting. The theory is that people who buy luxury goods, also have the means to pay the extra tax.

I truly believe that no one President or individual is able to run this country. Nor can one Party be a "fix all" for all our social and economic problems. We must get back to basics and make decisions that our forefathers intended for us to make. I believe the intent of the Constitution is clear:

"We the People of the United States, in Order to form a more perfect Union, establish Justice, insure domestic Tranquility, provide for the common defense, promote the general Welfare, and secure the Blessings of Liberty to ourselves and our Posterity, do ordain and establish this Constitution for the United States of America."

This Preamble to our Constitution illustrates that Government should have a role in these United States as representatives of the People. While these words do not in and of themselves promote any specific program, the intent is very clear and covers the major components of Government Spending. We will take a high level look at this now.

THE U.S. ECONOMY EXPOSED – Debt Crisis!

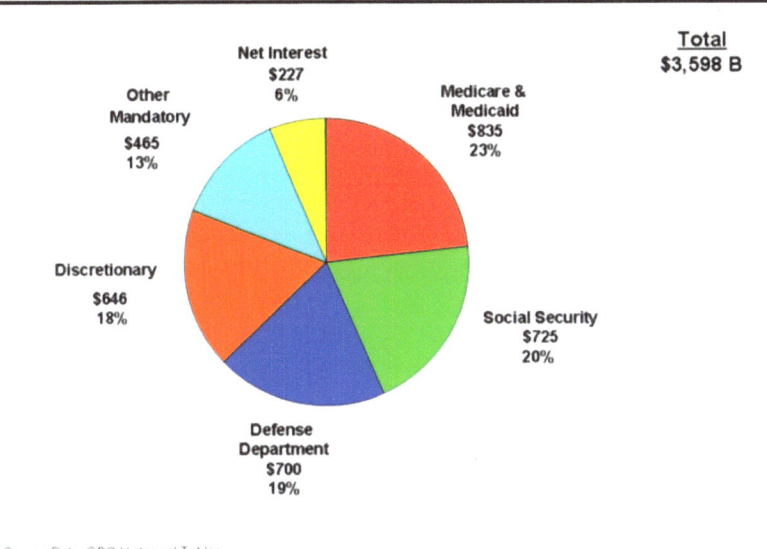

The majority (80%) of the spending is allocated in 4 major categories, Medicare/Medicaid, Social Security, Defense and Discretionary Spending. Depending on which Party is in power, dollars fluctuate between 18-22% among these categories, but not in Total. The spike in the cost of Social Health programs (23%) is due to ObamaCare.

The chart below illustrates how much the Government spends as a percent of GDP, contributing to a consistent 20% of GDP in good times and bad. We will always see a spike in Government spending during a recession and in times of war. In prosperous times, the Government may even spend less than 20% of GDP, as occurred during the Clinton years.

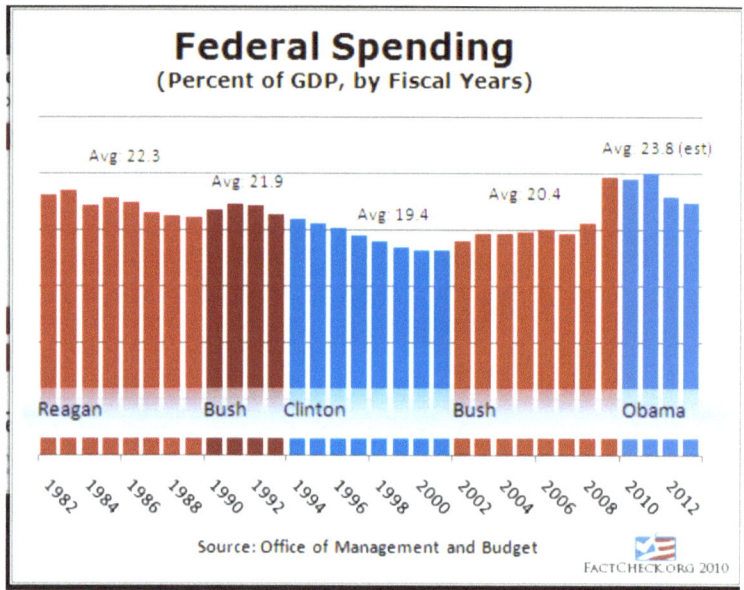

Because the other components of GDP are down, Government Spending is significantly up as a percent of GDP. This, however, does not mean that Government spending is totally out of control. It is not as depicted by this chart of annualized growth rate in real dollars by President.

THE U.S. ECONOMY EXPOSED – Debt Crisis!

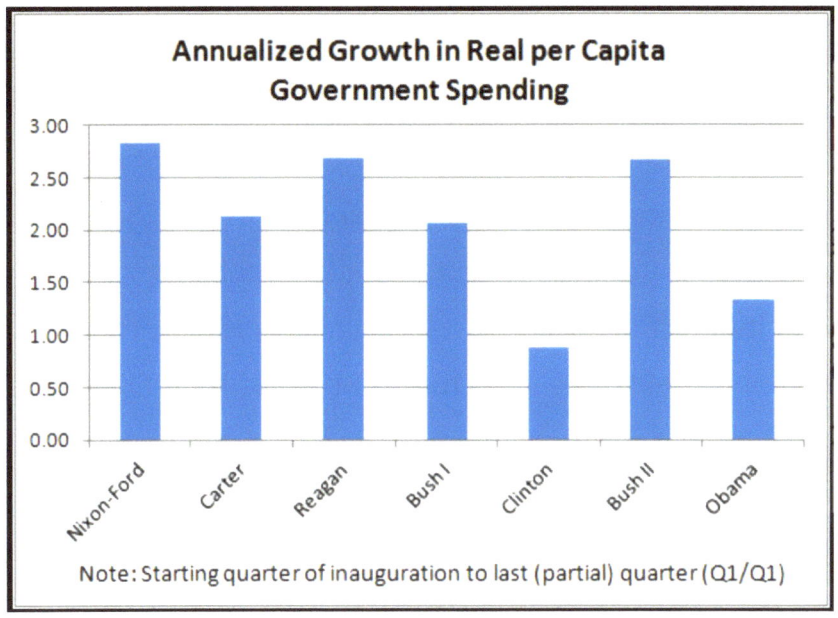

It seems clear that the Republicans spend more than the Democrats. A lot of this is due to the cost of War and Defense spending. The propaganda being thrown around each political party campaign is unbelievable with major twists and turns of the true facts. Numbers do lie when taken totally out of context. This is clearly what is happening during the 2012 election year.

There is no question that Romney and the Republicans were pushing for more tax cuts, the "free market" and increases in Defense spending. Romney is pro-business, more so than Obama, but record levels in Corporate Profits have not stimulated job hirings or increased salaries during the last few years. I am not convinced that we need lower taxes right now.

Obama's Democratic camp is on the opposite side of the spectrum, promoting a national healthcare system in the middle of a slow recovery period, the aging of America and the oncoming labor crisis. Clearly, all social spending programs need an overhaul to cover the incremental cost of healthcare. I am not sure that I want the Democrats to make these important long-term decisions right now.

So, where and when does the middle come to play! Congress will, most undoubtedly, play a critical role in U.S. economic policy. As I said earlier, the pendulum is swinging towards the middle, where the majority rules. The election was won by Obama with an improving job outlook and record corporation profits, along with the women and minority vote.

At this critical time, we need to deal with the gap between government revenues and expenses. When expenses exceed receipts, the Debt continues to grow. We cannot sustain the current Trillion dollar increases in U. S. Debt that we experienced over the last three years. Something has to give, and in my mind, we need a Balanced Budget Amendment that Congress passed during the Clinton years. Two decades of tax cuts does not balance a budget, especially during recessions.

What are the real numbers anyway? You only have to look at one chart . . . The comparison of Government Receipts and Expenditures to paint a clear picture.

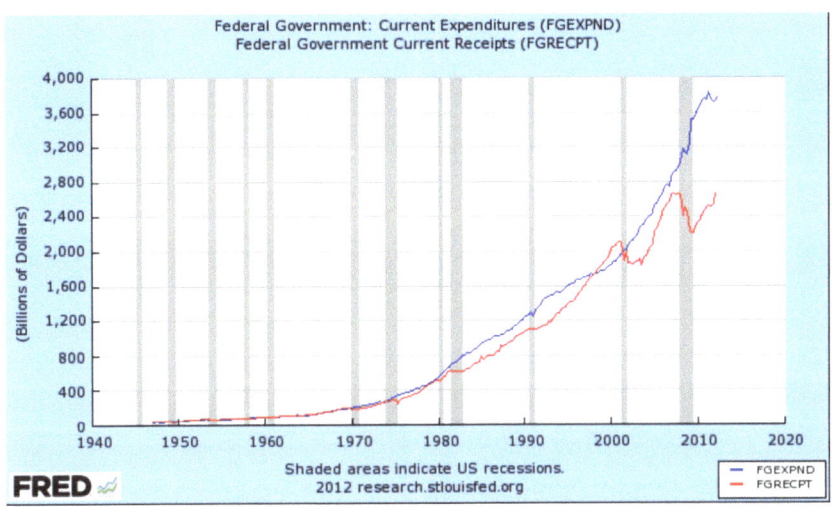

The gap between the lines needs to move back towards equilibrium. The Reagan/Bush I years from 1980 to 1992 had a major impact in the rise of The U.S. Debt. After the Clinton years of achieving a balanced budget from 1993 - 1996, the Bush II Administration continued the rise in our deficit spending and the tax cuts deployed during the recession exacerbated the Debt situation. With the collapse of the financial markets and the residential housing industry, Obama's bail-out programs really compounded the Debt situation.

Here is the current breakdown of our Deficit by Administration and WHO currently holds the bag of Debt:

How the U.S. Got $14 Trillion in Debt and Who Are the Creditors

$14.3 trillion

Who Holds the Debt		Amount	Amount	When the Debt Was Accumulated
The Public	Includes debt held by individuals, corporations, banks and insurance companies, pension and mutual funds, state and local governments.	3.6	2.4	**President Obama** (2009-11) Stimulus spending, tax cuts, and the effects of 2007-9 recession in lost revenues and automatic spending, like unemployment compensation.
Foreign Countries	China	1.2	6.1	**George W. Bush** (2001-9) Tax cuts, the wars in Iraq and Afghanistan, economic downturn in 2001 and recession starting in 2007.
	Japan	0.9		
	Britain			
	Oil-exporting countries			
	Other countries	1.9		
U.S. Gov't	FEDERAL RESERVE SYSTEM Includes collateral for U.S. currency and store of liquidity for emergency needs.	1.6	1.4	**Bill Clinton** (1993-2001) Despite two years of on-budget surpluses, deficit spending in other years added to the debt.
	SOCIAL SECURITY TRUST FUNDS Surpluses generated by the program that have been invested in government bonds.	2.7	1.5	**George Bush** (1989-93) The first gulf war and lower revenue from a recession.
			1.9	**Ronald Reagan** (1981-89) Peacetime defense spending and permanent tax cuts.
	OTHER GOV'T TRUST FUNDS	1.9	1.0	**Before Reagan** (1981 AND EARLIER) Deficit spending from wars and economic downturns.

These numbers were published in late-July 2012 collectively compiled by several branches of the Government, including the Department of Treasury, Financial Management Service, the Bureau of Public Debt, the Federal Reserve Bank of New York, and the Office of Management and Budget.

THE U.S. ECONOMY EXPOSED – Debt Crisis!

WHO DUNNIT? Since 1980, Republican policies and budgets have accounted for 67% of our $14 Trillion in Debt, or nearly $10 Trillion. What we have seen over the last 30 years is "trickle up" economics, nothing of the sort that the Republicans tout with their "trickle down" theory. The Rich keep getting richer, while Middle Class America continue to lose ground.

So, which Party is best to right-size the ship?

- If you believe that the U.S. should go to war to protect our interests around the world, want free markets to wheel and deal, and want to impose more tax cuts to stimulate growth, then the Republicans are the party of choice.

- If you believe that affordable healthcare is needed for America, want more government subsidies to help the poor make ends meet, and want to impose more taxes on the wealthy, then the Democrats are the clear choice.

- If you are a middle of the roader, like I am, and dislike the extremes of the Left-Wing and Right-Wing, we need a Bipartisan Congress to make the right choices at this critical juncture in U.S. history.

THE U.S. ECONOMY EXPOSED – Debt Crisis!

The numbers only lie when taken totally out of context. By taking this macroeconomic look at the economy, it should put things in perspective for you. Regardless, it takes two, and a whole lot of support from Congress, to Tango. COMPROMISE is the name of the game for the next 4 years. Both parties should be able to keep each other in check and limit extreme government spending policies.

In future editions of "The U.S. Economy Exposed" series, we will be updating these charts and modifying our assessment of the economy going forward. At times, we will expand our discussions on the individual components of GDP, inluding **C**onsumption + **I**nvestment + **G**overnment Spending + (**E**xports – i**M**ports). But, we expect to develop more detailed and more frequent discussions beginning in 2013 on our Website at http://US-Economy-Exposed.com, and to publish new editions annually in this series.

What I hope to accomplish over the next 5-10 years is to provide insight to small and medium-sized businesses in order to stimulate innovation and entrepreneurship through the analysis of economic trends and short-term forecasts. It would be great if my ideas are used by business to invest in the future growth of America.

About the Author

Keith Ouellette, ChFC, CLU

Financial Executive with over 35 years of experience in the financial services industry, primarily in the Life and Health insurance markets, as a General Manager/CFO of Third Party Administrators (TPAs), CFO of a Property & Casualty (Health and Non-Standard Auto) Insurer, an Insurance Regulator for two State Insurance Departments (FL and NC) and most recently, as a SOX, Internal Control and Compliance Specialist for an Insurance Company.

Performed financial exams, forensic audits, due diligence reviews, and small business valuations for acquisition analysis; coordinated development of Financial Work-Out Plans, assisted in turnarounds of financially-troubled companies and participated in financial analysis of companies targeted for potential mergers and acquisitions.

He has strong compassion for doing the right thing in times of trouble for small business and has studied the impact of economic indicators on future sales and costs. His unique perspective on looking at the big picture (macro approach) and developing specific solutions to problems in bad times (micro approach) has helped him formulate timely corrective action plans for companies.

You can visit his LinkedIn Profile at http://www.linkedin.com/in/keitheouellette for his analysis of current economic indicators and impact on current GDP trends.

www.ingramcontent.com/pod-product-compliance
Lightning Source LLC
Chambersburg PA
CBHW041109180526
45172CB00001B/178